CAR BADGES

This I-SPY book belongs to:_____

Introduction

Almost every car – as well as vans, trucks and buses – carries a logo that lets you know which company makes it. The usual positions for this are on the front 'grille' (the slatted opening allowing air in to cool the engine's radiator) or else on the bonnet. Most cars feature their logo on the back too, generally situated above the number plate.

On any car journey – or even a walk along a busy road, or through a car park – you might come across dozens of these little symbols. But what, exactly, do they all mean? Why is there a three-pointed star on Mercedes-Benz cars, or a lion on MAN trucks, or two little chevrons on Citroën vans? This I-Spy book tries to explain these marques. It helps you have fun on any journey by explaining many of the car brands you're likely to come across on British roads. As there have been more than 6500 different makes of car and commercial vehicle since 1885, we couldn't possibly include every one. But we have included the logo of most brands currently on UK sale (plus a few that are common in other countries,

and might be seen here occasionally), and several from classic marques which, while no longer manufactured, are still relatively common sights. It's quite difficult to spy some of the rarer car logos, because they are found on expensive sports and luxury cars of which only a handful are sold in Britain each year. On the other hand, we've also included the logos found on most of the commercial vehicles you'll come across. Don't let a truck or bus pass you by without checking if it could earn you I-Spy points!

By getting to know car logos, you'll understand more about the people who founded each car manufacturer, the places they come from, and sometimes the company's achievements or ambitions. If you thought logos were only found on clothes, electronic gadgets and food packaging then you're in for a few surprises!

How to use your I-SPY book

We've selected these logos to reflect the widest possible range of cars and commercial vehicles you're likely to spy across Britain. They're arranged in alphabetical order,

so you may need to memorise the logo as you hunt through the book to identify it if the make is not obvious from the badge.
You need 1000 points to send off for your I-Spy

certificate (see page 64) but there are masses of points in every book. As you make each I-Spy, write your score in the box.

ABARTH

You'll find this image of an aggressive scorpion on high-performance Fiats. Karl Abarth was an Austrian speed addict who first built racing cars and equipment in Italy in 1949. When he took Italian citizenship, he also changed his first name to Carlo; Fiat took over his firm in 1971. Abarth's birthday was 15 November, making his star sign Scorpio... and hence this scorpion.

I-SPY points: 25

Date: _____

AC

The initials stand for Auto Carriers, as the company now known for high-performance sports cars like the 1963 Cobra originally built three-wheeled Auto Carrier delivery trucks! When it moved into cars, the curved 'A' and 'C' were cast into the wheel hubs. Framed in a circle from 1925, they made a neat badge. AC has changed hands often, and still makes a few cars each year.

I-SPY points: 40

Date: _____

3

AIXAM

This is a French brand of ultra-small city cars that, in some cases, can be driven without a full car licence. The Aixam Mega is a tiny four-seater saloon offered with either a small petrol engine or battery-electric power. The capital 'M' in the car's badge has a pair of wings set across it but, oddly, the 'Aixam' word doesn't appear on the bodywork.

I-SPY points: 35

Date: _____

ALFA ROMEO

The coat of arms of the Italian city of Milan, where Alfa Romeo was founded in 1910, is the centrepiece. The red cross on the left salutes the local army's earliest crusade of 1095. The green serpent on the right dates back to the sixth century, when Germanic tribes conquered northern Italy; look closely and you'll see the beast is eating its foe – a man!

I-SPY points: 15

Date: _____

ARIEL

The capital 'A' depicted in the Ariel's badge is designed to look like a road stretching into the distance. This high-powered, two-seater fun car, which is built in a small factory in Somerset, is unusual in having no conventional bodywork; the chassis and frame of the car is fully exposed, while the mid-mounted engine comes from the Honda Civic Type-R. In the 1950s, Ariel was famous for its motorbikes.

I-SPY points: 45

Date: _____

ASTON MARTIN

Aston Martins have featured a 'winged' motif since 1932. It represents a scarab beetle in flight, wings outstretched, and reflects the 1930s craze for Egyptology. The design's been simplified several times since; the company's title unites the name of co-founder Lionel Martin, with Aston Clinton, a Buckinghamshire village where it had great success in the hillclimb competition up nearby Aston hill.

I-SPY points: 30

Date: _____

AUDI

The four inter-linked rings of the Audi logo are a neat pointer to the company's Quattro four-wheel drive system. But it actually originated in 1932, when four German carmakers – Audi, DKW, Horch and Wanderer – merged to form one, Auto Union. Only the DKW name survived after the Second World War, but Audi superseded it in 1965.

I-SPY points: 10

Date: _____

AUSTIN

Austins were popular British family cars built between 1905 and 1988. Several images were used, and our picture of an Austin A90 Atlantic from the early 1950s shows them all: at the top is a three-dimensional wheel with feathered wings; below that the company's signature script; at the bottom, the family coat-of-arms of company founder Herbert Austin. Score for any Austin logo you see.

I-SPY points: 25

Date: _____

AUSTIN-HEALEY

Austin-Healeys are some of the best-loved classic British sports cars, even though the last one was sold in 1971. The Austin and Healey companies joined forces to launch their first two-seater roadster in 1952. The logo they created for it followed others in framing the words with stylised bird's wing emblems to suggest swiftness. Differing slightly on each model, the logo generally features red enamel on a chrome base.

I-SPY points: 35

Date: _____

I-SPY points: 30

Date: _____

BENTLEY

One of the most elegant 'winged' badges you'll see on any car adorns the radiator grilles of Bentleys. On older cars, and some newer ones, you'll also see a three-dimensional Bentley mascot featuring a capital 'B' with wings outstretched behind it. Special models feature other colours like red, green and blue, but the usual style is a white 'B' on a black oval, with a chrome base.

7

BERTONE

Bertone isn't a make of car but an Italian company which designs and assembles cars for other companies' behalf. The oddly-shaped, lower-case 'b' looks like it's sitting on the prow of a three-dimensional object; look out for it on cars like the older Vauxhall Astra coupé and convertible, Fiat Punto convertible, and also on classics like the Lamborghini Countach, Lancia Stratos and Fiat X1/9.

I-SPY points: 30

Date: _____

BMW

BMW stands for Bayerische Motoren Werke or, in English, the Bavarian Motor Works . Before it started carmaking in 1928 it was famous for its aeroplane engines. Its logo does resemble the spinning blades of an aircraft propeller at speed reflecting the origins of the company but there is also conjecture that the blue-and-white pattern is derived from a section of the Bavarian state flag.

I-SPY points: 15

Date: _____

BRISTOL

The logo for these expensive British cars features the Bristol coat-of-arms because the cars are handbuilt in the West Country city. It's a shield showing a castle on a clifftop with, on the horizon, a ship sailing into port. The logo shown here is on an early car using one of Bristol's own engines; the '2-LITRE' part was dropped in 1961 when the company started using American-made power units.

I-SPY points: 35

Date: _____

BUGATTI

At 253mph, Bugatti's amazing Veyron is the fastest genuine production car on earth today, as well as one of the most expensive. It carries the marque's logo almost exactly as created by company founder Ettore Bugatti, in France in 1910. It's a perfect oval, and features Bugatti's personal monogram above the 'BUGATTI' name in white capitals and shadowed in black. The traditional Bugatti grille, as here, is always horseshoe-shaped.

I-SPY points: 50

Date: _____

9

I-SPY points: 35

Date: _____

BUICK

Buicks are traditional American cars, which means they tend to be large, powerful and luxurious. They are not sold in the UK, but a few find their way here, and you'll probably see one on any holiday in the USA. Since 1960, Buicks have featured three small shields on their logos. They were very loosely adapted from the family crest of David Buick, the company's Scottish founder.

CADILLAC

Frenchman Antoine de la Mothe Cadillac founded the American city of Detroit in 1701. The place would become the centre of US carmaking in the 20th century, and one of its most famous marques adopted not only Cadillac's name but also, for its logo, his family crest. Small numbers of Cadillacs are sold in the UK, and President Obama uses one as his official transport.

I-SPY points: 35

Date: _____

I-SPY points: 50

Date: _____

CAPARO

Unveiled in March 2006, the Caparo T1 is the flagship of a car parts manufacturer founded by India's Paul family. With amazing performance from its 575bhp V8 engine, the T1 looks more like a Formula 1 racer than the roadgoing car it is. The yellow-and-black striped logo is simply meant to reflect Caparo's futuristic technology. As only 24 are made each year, spying one driving around will be very unusual.

CATERHAM

Caterham's sports cars have been adored by keen drivers since 1973, when the Caterham, Surrey based company bought the design rights to the two-seater Super Seven from Lotus. Lotus's own logo was altered by upturning the familiar camshaft lobe shape. Inside this, the word 'SUPER' was arrayed above the figure '7' on a bright yellow background. The usual colour scheme is yellow and green on chrome.

I-SPY points: 35

Date: _____

CHEVROLET

The logo for this US-originated car brand is nicknamed the 'bowtie'. Louis Chevrolet was a Swiss racing driver, but it was businessman William Durant who made the company successful. He used to tell the tale that he noticed the bowtie shape on wallpaper in a Paris hotel, but in fact he copied it from the trademark for Coalette firelighters that he spotted in a newspaper advert!

I-SPY points: 20

Date: _____

CHRYSLER

The elaborate, old-fashioned logo for America's Chrysler cars was the idea of Walter Chrysler himself. He wanted it to look like the kind of rosette that might be seen pinned to prize-winning livestock because, when he started his firm in 1923, he thought that wealthy farmers were the best customers to target. The logo was dropped in 1962 but revived in 1998.

I-SPY points: 15

Date: _____

CITROËN

Citroën enthusiasts call this logo the 'double chevron'. It represents the precision-machined grooves on gear wheels, as these are what André Citroën manufactured before expanding into cars in 1919; Citroën gears were even fitted to the ill-fated liner Titanic. The double chevron is expressed in various ways on Citroën vehicles, and in 2008 was given a more rounded look. Citroën was once owned by Michelin.

I-SPY points: 10

Date:

COLEMAN MILNE

Located in Bolton, Lancashire, Coleman Milne is a specialist company that converts cars into stretched limousines and hearses. So you might see its small purple-and-gold roundel on a lengthened Saab or Mercedes-Benz used to transport celebrities – or even your town's mayor – or on an Australian-sourced Ford Fairlane hearse taking someone on their final journey. Funeral directors have been buying Coleman Milne hearses since the 1950s.

I-SPY points: 30

Date:

DACIA

The blue Dacia shield, with its rows of identical triangles in a lighter shade, could one day be a familiar sight in the UK. The company is Renault-owned, and Dacia's Logan saloon is liked for its simplicity and ruggedness. If you see one in the UK then the owner may well be on holiday here.

I-SPY points: 40

Date: _____

DAEWOO

It's pronounced 'Day-oo' and means, in Korean, 'the great universe'. Daewoos were sold in the UK between 1995 and 2004 – budget-priced family cars from South Korea. They originally came with an oval logo featuring six, white, fanned-out lines to represent the six continents, with the spaces at each end and in between signifying the seven oceans. The logo here is the later version in much simplified form.

I-SPY points: 20

Date: _____

DAF

You'll see these three capital letters on the front of many of the trucks delivering goods all over the UK. They stand for Doorne's Aanhangwagen Fabriek which, translated from the original Dutch, means Doorne's Trailer Factory. Although DAF originally made trailers – and once built small cars too – today it's one of Europe's biggest truck manufacturers, and has a factory in Leyland, Lancashire.

I-SPY points: 10

Date: _____

DAIHATSU

Daihatsu is one off Japan's smaller carmakers, although it has links to Toyota; its cars are 'niche' products like city cars, sports cars, 4x4 off-roaders and small delivery vans. It has a bold and simple logo, a capital 'D' tilted to the left and usually displayed in an oval frame. The word Daihatsu is a compound of the Japanese words for 'Osaka', where it's based, and 'motor'.

I-SPY points: 15

Date: _____

DAIMLER

This is the oldest British car marque, having been founded in 1896 as a branch of the German Daimler company. Yet the stylish logo you see here was first attached to a Daimler in 1960: before that time, the cars didn't have one at all, and were identifiable only by their fluted radiator grille frame. Today's Daimlers are upmarket versions of Jaguar saloons.

I-SPY points: 20

Date: _____

DE TOMASO

The blue-and-white striped background to the De Tomaso logo is the Argentine flag and the black T-shape symbolises a branding iron. It salutes the ancestry of Alejandro de Tomaso's family as cattle ranchers in the Andes. De Tomaso's cars were rare, fast and beautiful machines, and they were built in Modena, Italy. Very few have been made, so they're an unusual 'spy' on UK roads.

I-SPY points: 45

Date: _____

DODGE

This evocation of a big-horn ram was first seen on Dodge vehicles in 1932, shortly after Walter Chrysler took control of the American make. He liked the way the 'king of the trail' animal summed up toughness. After a period in the wilderness, the ram livery returned to Dodges from the early 1990s, and today you'll find it on all its cars, like this Challenger, and pick-up trucks.

I-SPY points: 20

Date: _____

FERRARI

In a British poll conducted in 2009, Ferrari's prancing black horse logo was voted the 'most iconic' in the world. It first appeared as a lucky charm on the side of Enzo Ferrari's race team cars in the 1930s. The bright yellow is the traditional colour for Modena, where the cars are built. On Ferrari competition cars, the initials 'SF' are sometimes added; they stand for 'Scuderia Ferrari', meaning 'Team Ferrari'.

I-SPY points: 30

Date: _____

FIAT

Fiat has changed the logo on its cars many times over the years, and the very latest one is actually a return to a design used between 1959 and 1966. One feature, however, has remained pretty much intact since 1901, and that's the unique capital 'A' with the right-hand stem kinked inwards. Fiat is actually an acronym, standing or Fabbrica Italiana Automobili Torino (Italian Automobile Factory of Turin).

I-SPY points: 10

Date: _____

FODEN

For 150 years between 1856 and 2006, Cheshire-based Foden made working machines for British business, first steam engines and then trucks. Although no longer manufactured, there are still thousands of large Foden vehicles on British roads, with their flowing 'Foden' script in a four pointed star as a logo on the front. They're generally articulated trucks or eight-wheel tippers.

I-SPY points: 20

Date: _____

I-SPY points: 10

Date: _____

FORD

Often referred to as the 'blue oval', the Ford logo is one of the most familiar in Britain, as its cars and vans have been best-sellers here for decades. The curly, silver script was designed by Childe Harold Wills, an assistant to Henry Ford, in 1903. He used a home printing press he had in his attic...the same machine he'd used as a teenager to make pocket money by printing and selling calling cards to friends and neighbours.

I-SPY points: 40

Date: _____

FSO

FSO cars were, in the 1970s and '80s, quite popular here because they were cheap. Built in Communist-era Poland, these Fiat-engined cars always trailed western European standards of design and performance. The circular logo looks rather like a gunsight. FSO stands for Fabryka Samochodów Osobowych (literal translation: Factory for Passenger Automobiles). They're rare to see because most in the UK have been scrapped.

19

GHIA

You'll find this little emblem on the side window pillars of the top luxury model in most Ford ranges (this is a Mondeo). The lettering is a rendering of the signature of Italian car bodywork designer Giacinto Ghia. From 1919, his company was renowned for its stylish coachwork – most famously for the Volkswagen Karmann-Ghia. Ford bought the design house in 1973, and has used its trademark to this day.

I-SPY points: 15

Date: _____

GINETTA

Ginetta is one of several small British sports car manufacturers, and its many different models of two-seaters have been popular with road and track drivers since it opened for business in 1958. The triangulated 'G' on a yellow circle makes for a simple logo, but a mystery remains. The four Walklett brothers who started the company have never revealed where the inspiration for the Ginetta name came from.

I-SPY points: 40

Date: _____

HEULIEZ

I-SPY points: 30

Date:

Logo hunters will really need to keep a careful eye out for this example, showing a capital 'H' just in front of a cartwheel. It's to be found on the front wings of the Vauxhall Tigra. The reason is that this car, together with its clever, metal folding top, is built for Vauxhall by France's Heuliez factory. Heuliez can trace its roots back to when most vehicles were horse-drawn.

HINO

Despite being squeezed into an elliptic frame, this chrome logo is just about recognisable as a capital 'H', for Hino. The firm is a division of Toyota, and is Japan's leading truck firm, making a wide range of medium- and heavy-duty trucks for trade and industry. However, many of the ones you'll come across on British roads are assembled in Ireland.

I-SPY points: 20

Date:

HONDA

The prominent 'H' on the front of all Hondas means there's no mistaking any of its cars. The uprights of the 'H' are splayed out slightly, and it's sometimes displayed on a red background, although mostly it uses a black one. The popular Civic, Jazz and CR-V are all British-made. Honda motorbikes have a different logo, featuring a large, single bird's wing above the word 'HONDA'.

I-SPY points: 10

Date: _____

I-SPY points: 35

Date: _____

HUMMER

The massive Hummer off-roaders don't have a logo as such; the tough, high-riding sport-utility vehicles simply spell out the marque name on the front in heavy-set capital letters. The Hummer, derived from a large American military truck.

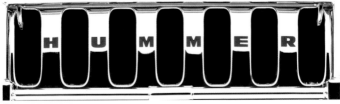

HYUNDAI

In contrast to Honda, Hyundai uses a strange slanted 'H' on the front of its cars, worn as an entirely chrome decoration. It was first seen in 1991. Hyundais come from South Korea, where they have been produced since 1974, and have been sold in the UK since 1982. The range today spans everything from city cars to large people carriers, and most things in between.

I-SPY points: 10

Date:

INFINITI

Infiniti cars are recent arrivals in the UK – so likely to be a rare sight here – although they've been sold in the USA since the 1980s. They are not, in fact, American but a range of sports and luxury models built by Nissan in Japan. The elliptical logo has a feature at its base that tapers to a sharp point, clearly suggesting the never-ending road towards infinity.

I-SPY points: 30

Date:

23

INVICTA

Launched in 2002 (but reviving a British sports car name famous in the 1930s), the Invicta S1 was one of the world's first cars with carbon-fibre composite bodywork. It remains very rare, so seeing one will be quite an event! The logo on the front originated in 1933. It has the 'INVICTA' word stacked vertically at the centre, flanked by exotic plumage, the feathers picked out in green, blue and red enamel.

I-SPY points: 50

Date: _____

ISUZU

Just so long as you can read then you'll always be able to recognise an Isuzu, as no graphic attempt has been made to spice up the simple 'ISUZU' lettering these vehicles carry on their radiator grilles. Isuzu is another of Japan's smaller manufacturers, this time concentrating on pick-up trucks and 4x4 vehicles. Isuzu also makes larger delivery trucks that are increasingly popular in the UK.

I-SPY points: 20

Date: _____

24

IVECO

Vans and trucks made by IVECO are a common sight in this country. Although the Industrial Vehicle Corporation, which is shortened to IVECO, is part of the Italian Fiat organisation, it has factories all over Europe, where it's one of the biggest makers of commercial vehicles. It has no logo other than the spelling of its name, which sits boldly on the front of its trucks, vans and minibuses.

I-SPY points: 10

Date: _____

JAGUAR

The symbol of a pouncing jaguar is known, in Jaguar circles, as 'the leaper'. It has been used, in various forms, ever since the sports and luxury car company introduced the Jaguar name in 1935. Most Jaguars also sport a bonnet badge showing the growling face of the big cat from south America. Older examples of the cars often have a three-dimensional bonnet mascot of a pouncing Jaguar.

I-SPY points: 15

Date: _____

I-SPY points: 15

Date: _____

JEEP

If you know anything about fonts then you might recognise the 'Jeep' logo as being in Franklin Gothic. That's the way it's always written on these four-wheel drive family cars from the USA. The original GP, standing for General Purpose, was developed as a battlefield taxi for the Second World War, when soldiers began to slur the initials into the word "jeep". It finally became an official trademark in 1950.

JENSEN

Jensen's most famous car was the Interceptor, a four-seater luxury model introduced in 1966 and winning admiration for its Aston Martin-like image and performance. The Jensen logo was another winged wonder; as seen on the car's long bonnet, it featured on a badge richly enamelled in red and cream. You also score if you see the more intricate 'wing' logo on earlier Jensens like the C-V8 or 541.

I-SPY points: 30

Date: _____

I-SPY points: 25

Date: _____

KARMANN

Keep a sharp eye out for the shield-shaped logo of German coachbuilder Karmann. The firm builds convertible cars for large car companies, but you will only see this logo on convertible Renaults like the 19 and last two generations of Megane. Karmann's open-top version of the Volkswagen Golf also has it moulded into the roll-over frame, but the classic Karmann-Ghia features only 'KARMANN' wording.

I-SPY points: 10

Date: _____

KIA

Kia has been selling more and more cars to British drivers, especially since the South Korean manufacturers opened a European plant on Slovakia. The current oval Kia logo has graced all its cars since 1996. In raised chrome with a black background, it features an unusual capital 'A' that does without the usual crossbar. It's shown here on the Soul family model.

KOENIGSEGG

Christian von Koenigsegg was
just 22 when he decided to build
a Swedish supercar that would
compete with Ferrari. It took
him eight years but, in 2002, the
amazing, 240mph Koenigsegg
CC8S was launched to rave
reviews. Just a handful has been
sold in the UK, but if you see one
it will bear this logo on the front.
It's Christian's own interpretation
of the von Koenigsegg family
crest, which dates back to the
16th century.

I-SPY points: 50

Date: _____

I-SPY points: 25

Date: _____

LADA

Russia's gigantic Lada factory,
600 miles south-east of Moscow,
doesn't export many of its cars
to the west any more; when it
did, they found a ready market
because they were robust and
cheap. The Viking longboat image
on the cars' logo commemorates
the fact that there was once a
Norse invasion in the region the
factory occupies. Few British-
registered Ladas have escaped
the crusher.

LAGONDA

This is the name Aston Martin has, in the past, given to luxury saloon cars it offers. The last of those was made in 1991, but now the company intends to relaunch Lagonda in an attempt to rival expensive limousines from Bentley, Maybach and Rolls-Royce. Here is the new logo they'll be using, a modern rendition of Lagonda's 1930s 'wings' design. You can score for absolutely any Lagonda you encounter!

I-SPY points: 45

Date: _____

LAMBORGHINI

Millionaire industrialist Ferruccio Lamborghini, it's said, vowed to make better supercars than Ferrari and – with the stunning Lamborghini Miura, Countach, Diablo and Gallardo – the two marques are certainly neck-and-neck for driving excitement. Lambo's logo sought to outdo Ferrari too, with a charging bull instead of Ferrari's bucking stallion. Signor Lamborghini chose this because he was born under the star sign Taurus, for the bull.

I-SPY points: 40

Date: _____

LANCIA

Lancia's shield-shaped logo has been around as long as the upmarket Italian cars themselves – that is, since 1908. So has the dark blue colour and the suggestion of a four-spoke steering wheel. Lancia has built some fantastic cars in its 100-plus years – including the rally-winning Delta Integrale – but they're not currently sold in the UK, so any example you spot will either be owned by a collector or a tourist.

I-SPY points: 30

Date: _____

LAND ROVER

First revealed in 1948, the four-wheel drive Land Rover has always featured an oval logo with the 'LAND' and 'ROVER' words linked by a zig-zag hyphen. Oddly, the marque has never used a hyphen on its title but, until 1984, its vehicle badging did have one. The Land Rover logo today is always seen in green with cream lettering, zig-zag and outline.

I-SPY points: 10

Date: _____

30

LDV

LDVs are small- to medium-sized delivery vans and pick-up trucks that are widely used all over Britain. Many schools operate an LDV minibus, and the Royal Mail has a large fleet of them. The letters stand for Leyland DAF Vans, as the Birmingham manufacturer was once part of DAF and, before that, British Leyland. Sadly, in the recession of 2009, LDV closed down.

I-SPY points: 15

Date:

LEXUS

According to Lexus, the Japanese luxury car marque, the logo 'signifies the company's ever-expanding technological advancement and the limitless opportunities which lie ahead'. That is the message behind what most people would describe as a large capital 'L' framed by an ellipse. Lexus cars are actually made by Toyota, which launched this high end brand in 1989 to match BMW, Mercedes-Benz and Jaguar for comfort and style.

I-SPY points: 15

Date:

LIGIER

Like Aixam, the Ligier is a French-built microcar popular with drivers wanting low running costs or compact dimensions. It's classed as a 'quadricycle' for tax purposes so can be driven on a motorbike licence. Ligier was founded by former Formula 1 team owner Guy Ligier. That's why the tiny cars have crossed flags as a logo, one the French flag and the other the chequered flag from a race finish!

I-SPY points: 35

Date: _____

LINCOLN

Founded in 1920 and named after American president Abraham Lincoln, this is Ford's luxury car division. Its large, impressive products are very rarely found outside the USA, so you will be lucky to see one on British roads. Lincolns first boasted a heraldic crest in 1942, although it was totally made up by Ford's graphic designers. The only part of that crest that remains today is a four-pointed star, set across a four-sided shape.

I-SPY points: 45

Date: _____

LOTUS

The Lotus logo, always presented in a yellow circle, is a green, vaguely triangular shape that looks like a camshaft lobe in a high-performance engine. It always carries a monogram at the top above the 'LOTUS' name; this combination of A, C, B and C stands for Anthony Colin Bruce Chapman, the man who founded the Norfolk sports car maker back in 1947.

I-SPY points: 25

Date: _____

LTI

LTI Vehicles, the name of the company that builds the only purpose built iconic 'black cab' synonymous with London life. The current model is known as the TX4, and is the latest in a long line of taxis made by LTI and its forerunners specially designed to cope with London's narrow streets and vast area. But the TX4 can also be found in cities around the world.

I-SPY points: 15

Date: _____

MAN

The animal depicted in the logo on MAN trucks is the Brunswick lion. It's used because MAN took over a rival truckmaker in 1971, confusingly called Büssing, and the lion was Büssing's badge. The trucks were sold under the MAN-Büssing name until 1974, after which just the MAN name and the Büssing logo survived. MAN stands for 'Maschinenfabrik Augsburg Nurnberg', or the Machinery Factories of Augsburg & Nurnberg. It's the oldest company on the German stock market.

I-SPY points: 15

Date: _____

MARCOS

With the word 'MARCOS' in a blue oval at its centre, a contrasting, diagonal red stripe, and the background as a white flash, the Marcos logo makes an impact and signifies the fact these rare classic sports cars are thoroughly British. Although not currently being manufactured, they've been road and track favourites since 1959. Marcos is a compound of the founders' names: Jem MAR-sh and Frank COS-tin.

I-SPY points: 40

Date: _____

MASERATI

Neptune, the legendary nautical god, brandished his three-pronged trident to command the waves. There's a bronze sculpture of him in a fountain in Bologna's Piazza Del Nettuno, and this inspired the Maserati brothers to adopt the trident as their logo back in 1926. It's been found on Maserati cars ever since, and features on the front, back and sides of today's GranTurismo and Quattroporte models.

I-SPY points: 35

Date: _____

MAYBACH

The Maybach 57 and 62 were created by Mercedes-Benz in 2002 as the epitome in super-luxury limousines. They are often owned by celebrities. On their imposing bonnets, under which reside powerful V12 engines, they carry a three-dimensional version of the Maybach logo, which consists of two inter-linked capital 'Ms'. They stand for 'Maybach Manufaktur'. The original Maybach was built between 1921 and 1941.

I-SPY points: 45

Date: _____

MAZDA

The V-shape in the middle of Mazda's logo spreads out like an opening fan, representing, the Japanese company says: 'the creativity, the sense of mission, the resoluteness and vitality of Mazda'. Poised like wings ready to fly, the 'V' is also a starting point for future growth'. It was introduced in 1997, so older Mazdas carry different symbols; score for any that you spy.

I-SPY points: 10

Date: _____

MCLAREN

Mclaren has been most well-known, until now, for its Formula 1 racing team – a mainstay of the sport for decades. It also made the rare 231mph F1 road car in 1993. But the Woking-based company now plans to take on the Ferrari 458 and Porsche 911 with its mid-engined MP4-12C. So expect to see more of its red, boomerang-like 'speedmark' logo in wealthier parts of the country.

I-SPY points: 50

Date: _____

MERCEDES-BENZ

The three-pointed star emblem has been a design feature on Mercedes-Benz cars and trucks since about 1910. Today, you'll find it as a freestanding bonnet ornament, a large chrome cut-out, and as an enamel badge picked out in blue with a laurel wreath around its edge. The three points symbolise air, water and land, the three transport areas for which the company made engines in its early days.

I-SPY points: 10

Date: _____

MERCURY

You're not going to see many Mercury cars in the UK, as they have never been sold here; any that have crept in will be personal imports or, possibly, owned by US military personnel. In the USA, though, they are a popular, sporty line of cars made and sold by Ford. Since 1985, Mercurys have carried this logo showing the three stems of a capital 'M'.

I-SPY points: 40

Date: _____

METROCAB

Metrocab tried to rethink the classic London taxi in 1986. The main difference was a plastic body instead of a steel one, so it would be rust-free and cheap to repair. The Metrocab venture changed ownership several times. Most Metrocabs you'll see in London and other British cities have this logo, featuring a winged 'H' emblem from when the company was owned by Hooper & Co. The final Metrocabs were built in 2005.

I-SPY points: 20

Date: _____

MG

MG stands for Morris Garages, the sales network of Oxford-based carmaker Morris that came up with the idea for an affordable sports car using existing Morris parts. The distinctive, octagonal logo was created by MG accountant Edmund Lee, a talented amateur artist, in 1923. It first appeared on a car in 1928, and its traditional colour scheme is brown on cream. MG is now Chinese-owned.

I-SPY points: 15

Date: _____

MICHELIN

The famous 'Michelin Man' was created in 1898 after Edouard Michelin remarked, about a stack of differently sized tyres, that '...if it had arms it would look like a man'. He was named 'Bibendum' when his brother André spotted a character in a German beer advert announcing "Nunc est bibendum" – Latin for: "Now is the time to drink". Look out for him on the tyres of the cars you spy everywhere and also as a mascot mounted on trucks.

I-SPY points: 10

Date: _____

MINI

A prominent chrome 'MINI', set against a black circle, with four chrome bars descending in size, forming the simple wings either side. It's a typically British car logo. The Austin and Morris Minis were launched in 1959, Mini became a marque in its own right in 1969, and gained its first proper badge – an earlier version of this one – in 1997.

I-SPY points: 10

Date: _____

MITSUBISHI

This trademark first appeared in the 1870s on a Japanese ship owned by Yataro Iwasaki. He used it to honour his mentors, the powerful Toso clan, whose family crest contained three oak leaves, Iwasaki's own crest included three stacked diamonds and the whole resembled a three bladed ship's propeller. Mitsubishi is Japanese for 'three diamonds'. The company part-founded Japan's NYK shipping line, and diversified into cars in 1960.

I-SPY points: 15

Date: _____

MORGAN

The Morgan 4/4 is the longest-surviving car model ever. First introduced in 1936, you can still buy one in 2010! The logo has also sailed through these 74 years pretty much untouched. 'MORGAN' sits on a black cross as a centrepiece, with an elaborate plumage of wings outstretched behind it. Morgans are sports cars handbuilt in Malvern, Worcester, and the company is still entirely family-owned.

I-SPY points: 30

Date: _____

MORRIS

This logo features an ox crossing
a ford, apparently hinting
at the British city from which
the cars hailed. It was actually
taken from Oxford's coat of arms.
Indeed, the Morris Oxford was a
popular model, but you're most
likely to see the logo on the many
Morris Minors still in everyday
use – it was the first British car
to reach a million sales. The last
Morris was sold in 1984.

I-SPY points: 25

Date:

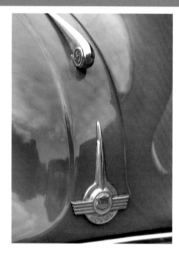

MYCAR

This logo was created by the
Hong Kong-based MyCar
founders in 2003. It's composed
of two letters, the inner one a 'T'
standing for technology while
the bar to the left is an 'I', for
innovation. The 'I' also suggests a
graphic path linking the two, via
which the MyCar was born. It's an
electric city car, noteworthy for
its Italian design and styling.

I-SPY points: 45

Date:

NISSAN

The 'NISSAN' name in black
capitals appears in a bar set across
a circle and, on the car, the whole
logo is reproduced in chrome.
It's a little similar to the style
of station signs on the London
Underground. The logo derives
from early Nissan corporate
identity that showed the circle in
red, to signify Japan's national
motto of being 'the land of the
rising sun'.

I-SPY points: 10

Date: _____

NOBLE

Lee Noble is the British designer
behind several two-seater,
high-performance sports cars.
The Noble bears his name even
though he no longer has anything
to do with the organisation that
makes it. His surname appears
in thin black capitals across a
simple yellow rectangle on the
front of cars like this M12 coupé,
which features a Ford V6 engine
mounted behind the driver and
passenger.

I-SPY points: 45

Date: _____

OLDSMOBILE

There's a slim chance you might see one of these large American cars on a British street, but you'll definitely see plenty in the USA because, between 1901 and 2004, over 35 million Oldsmobiles were sold. General Motors finally decided to axe the brand because Americans found it old-fashioned and dull. The logo represents a rocket on take-off, an image Oldsmobile first adopted in 1948.

I-SPY points: 40

Date: _____

OPEL

Opel is the brand name used all over Europe by General Motors – in fact, everywhere except the UK, where the same cars are sold as Vauxhall. The chrome logo consists of a lightning flash across a circle; it dates back to 1962 when the previous logo, showing a torpedo flashing across a circle, was updated. A small number of Opels do end up in Britain, so look out for them.

I-SPY points: 25

Date: _____

PAGANI

This cast metal logo is found on the exotic Pagani supercars that come from Modena in Italy. Horacio Pagani is the man behind these hugely fast and powerful two-seaters that compete with Ferraris and Lamborghinis. Pagani only builds a few dozen cars annually whereas Ferrari manufacture is in the thousands. The C12 made its debut in 1999, and features a mid-mounted Mercedes-Benz V12 engine.

I-SPY points: 50

Date: _____

PANTHER

The intricate wire mesh grille usually found on pre-war British sports cars forms the main part of the Panther logo, along with the traditional 'winged' element. Panthers were made between 1972 and 1990, and were usually entirely styled along the lines of 1930s models. They're all pretty rare but you might see one of the Vauxhall-engined Limas or Ford-powered Kallistas, perhaps at a classic car show.

I-SPY points: 40

Date: _____

PERODUA

The elliptical logo on this range
of economy cars imported from
Malaysia is split diagonally
across the centre into green
and red sections. The chrome
divider suggests the silhouette
of a capital 'P'; however, it is just
possible to visualise it as the
profile of a leaping deer, as this
was what formed the Perodua
logo until 2000, whereupon it was
remodelled into today's version.

I-SPY points: 20

Date: _____

PEUGEOT

A fierce roaring lion with
claws drawn, has featured in
standalone, cut-out form on
every Peugeot since 1975. On
recent models, it's become even
more prominent. Peugeot's lion,
however, dates right back to
1858 when one of the French
company's main products were
saw blades. The shape of the saw
handle, plus the sharpness of the
teeth, inspired the adoption of
the lion symbol.

I-SPY points: 10

Date: _____

PININFARINA

Here's another logo belonging not to a manufacturer but a car design company. Italy's Pininfarina styles and assembles cars for other companies, lately including Ferrari, Peugeot, Alfa Romeo and Volvo. It was founded by Battista 'Pinin' Farina. He changed his name in 1961, combining nickname and surname, but Pininfarina-designed and/or -built cars often carry a blue-and-red 'f' crest above the distinctive Pininfarina script.

I-SPY points: 25

Date:

PLYMOUTH

Between 1928 and 2001, Plymouth was a sister car marque to Chrysler, named after the English pilgrims who were first to colonise North America. That's why the early logo, which was reintroduced for the last six years of Plymouth's existence, features the pilgrims' ship, the Mayflower. There are a few Plymouths in the UK, mostly older models owned by American classic car fanatics. Score for any Plymouth you see.

I-SPY points: 40

Date:

46

PORSCHE

Like its sports car rival Ferrari,
Porsche also features a prancing
black horse in its logo. That's
because it's a central component
of the Stuttgart city coat-of-
arms from which the logo draws
heavily. In the Middle Ages,
Stuttgart was the site of a stud
farm (that is what the word
actually means in German). The
'PORSCHE' name, in square-cut
capitals is familiar on the cars too.

PONTIAC

Pontiac is yet another American
make of car recently made
obsolete. General Motors decided
to give Pontiac the chop in 2009
after 83 years. Its logo was a silver
star on a red arrowhead. It was
used to commemorate the chief of
the Ottawa Indians, who led the
rebellion against British settlers
in 1763. Pontiac built some cool
cars, but few were sold in the UK.

I-SPY points: 40

Date: _____

I-SPY points: 30
Date: _____

PROTON

The tiger is the national animal of Malaysia in much the same way that the bulldog is for Britain. As Protons are Malaysian-built, they sport a tiger's head motif on their logos. It is depicted in a yellowish-gold on a green circle, framed within a blue shield. Proton cars have been built in Malaysia since 1985, and the company is also the current owner of Britain's Lotus.

I-SPY points: 15

Date: _____

I-SPY points: 25, double points for a Reliant Scimitar, their iconic 4-wheel sports car.

Date: _____

RELIANT

Reliants were once a familiar sight on Britain's roads as they were the country's most popular three-wheeled economy cars. Although none have been made since 2000, you do still see them trundling along; plastic bodywork means they don't succumb to rust. The logo is a geometric representation of an eagle, usually seen in silver on a black background, bearing the 'RELIANT' name.

RENAULT

The large chrome diamond on all Renault cars, vans and trucks is easy to spot. A diamond-shaped emblem, originally with the word 'RENAULT' set across it, first appeared in 1925. At that time, Renaults were unusual in not having a traditional radiator grille, but the diamond-framed opening in the cars' nose panel acted as an outlet for the sound of the innovative electric horn behind it.

I-SPY points: 10

Date: _____

I-SPY points: 30

Date: _____

REVA

If you live in London then you're more likely to see this emblem, an 'R' in a circle, than anywhere else in Britain. That's because it's on the front of the Indian-made Reva G-Wiz electric car, a tiny two-seater that's been very popular with London residents and commuters because it emits zero emissions, and benefits from free parking and no Congestion Charge fees.

I-SPY points: 30

ROVER

It was a sad day for British car enthusiasts when Rover ceased trading in 2005, ending 101 years of carmaking, and closing the company's 100-year old Longbridge factory. It also meant goodbye to Rover's logo, a front-on representation of a Viking longship with a Viking warrior figurehead on its prow. Rover registered it as a trademark in 1930 because the idea of unstoppable invaders sat well with the car's reputation for reliable motoring.

ROLLS-ROYCE

The double-'R's in a rectangle celebrate the partnership between engineer Henry Royce and businessman Charles Rolls. It eventually led to both luxurious and expensive Rolls-Royce cars and some of the world's best aircraft engines. Up to 1930, the logo was always red-on-chrome, whereupon it was changed to black; however, red is sometimes used for limited edition cars. The Rolls-Royce radiator mascot is officially called 'The Spirit of Ecstasy'.

I-SPY points: 10

SAAB

The Saab logo, featuring the head of the mythical half-lion half-eagle griffin, is an oddity. It's there because Saab and truckmaker Scania were part of the same, large Swedish company. In 1987, bosses decided to ditch Saab's old aeroplane logo and adopt Scania's griffin for both cars and lorries. So, today, Saabs carry Scania's logo even though the two vehicles are no longer connected in any way.

I-SPY points: 15

Date: _____

I-SPY points: 15

Date: _____

SCANIA

This is a large commercial vehicle company, based in Sweden and now controlled by Volkswagen. It builds a range of heavy trucks and chassis for coaches, so you are most likely to see Scanias on the motorway. The griffin, half-lion and half-eagle, comes from the crest for the Skane district of southern Sweden, where Scania is based. The logo is usually positioned at the top right of the vehicle's grille.

SEAT

You pronounce it "Say-at" but the word actually stands for Sociedad Espanola de Automoviles de Turismo... or the Spanish Passenger Car Company. This style of distinctive capital 'S' as a logo has been around since 1998, and you'll generally see it as a large chrome emblem bordered in black. Seat is the biggest carmaker in Spain, where it was established in 1953 initially with the assistance of FIAT, but is today part of Volkswagen.

I-SPY points: 15

Date: _____

SEDDON ATKINSON

These trucks have been around since 1970, when the rival Seddon and Atkinson truck-making firms in Lancashire merged. It was the Atkinson logo that won through, though – a big capital 'A' framed in a circle. The company is now part of IVECO and its UK plant shut down, but the brand name lives on, usually found on specialist vehicles for local councils, like refuse collectors.

I-SPY points: 20

Date: _____

SKODA

If it wasn't for the importance of its name, this would be one of the most unusual logos you'll find on any car. First registered in 1924, it's actually supposed to show the feathers of an American Indian's head-dress, along with an arrow. It hints at the fact Skoda, based in the Czech Republic, originally made armaments, and the 'eye' on the feathers was added to suggest vision.

I-SPY points: 10

Date: _____

SMART

The Smart car first came along in 1997 as a joint venture between the company that created the Swatch watch and Daimler-Benz. Their concept was to produce an extremely short, economical and stylish city runabout. The current logo first appeared in 2002. It's a so-called 'pictogram' of a circle whose right-hand side is formed of a triangular arrow pointing outwards, and on the cars themselves it has a brushed aluminium finish.

I-SPY points: 15

Date: _____

I-SPY points: 50

Date:

SPYKER

The exclusive Spyker C8 sports car, built in Holland, was unveiled in 2000, but the make's first era of carmaking was between 1900-25. In those days, it was also in the aeroplane business, and hence the logo mixes an aircraft propeller and a spoked car wheel. Arrayed around the lower part of the wheel is Spyker's Latin motto: 'NULLA TENACI INVIA EST VIA' – 'nothing is insuperable to the tenacious'.

SSANGYONG

SsangYong means two dragons, and these are apparently represented in this logo. Legend has it that two dragons wanted to return to the skies but the 'skymaster' would only admit one of them. They refused to be parted and so agreed neither would enter. Suitably impressed, the skymaster relented and let them both in. The most popular SsangYong is the Rexton 4x4, in a range of useful and roomy vehicles from South Korea.

I-SPY points: 20

Date:

SUBARU

Subaru's logo is an oval with six, four-pointed stars inside it, one large one to the left and five smaller, identically-sized ones to the right. It has special resonance in Japan because it symbolises the star cluster Pleiades, in the Taurus constellation, which is a traditional feature in Japanese culture and literature. Indeed, 'subaru' means six stars in modern-day Japanese.

I-SPY points: 15

Date: _____

SUZUKI

Suzuki's spiky, compressed rendering of a capital 'S', in three parallel strokes, simply stands for Suzuki – that's as complex as it gets! The Suzuki Motor Corporation grew out of a family owned loom-making business before diversifying into cars and motor bikes. Suzuki is one of the most common surnames in the Kanto region, which includes Tokyo, and the company's still controlled by the founding Suzuki family.

I-SPY points: 15

Date: _____

TALBOT

A capital 'T' in a circle – generally used as a plastic, silver-on-black radiator grille badge – means you've just spied a Talbot. It's likely to be a rare sight. Although the name dates back to the Earl of Shrewsbury & Talbot's carmaking activities in 1903, it was revived between 1979-86. Those 1980s Talbots like the Horizon and Samba sold badly, and most by now have gone to the scrapyard.

I-SPY points: 30

Date:

TATA

The Tata Nano is one of the most talked-about new cars in years. It offers four doors and four seats for just £1300 in India, where it's made, and promises to provide the first taste of motoring for many Indian families. Its logo looks like a chrome T-junction. You won't see one in the UK yet, but there are a handful of Tata's big, tough pick-ups on our roads.

I-SPY points: 30

Date:

TATRA

Tatra, of the Czech Republic, once made the big limousines the country's leaders rode around in when the country was under Russian communist control. Today, though, the firm is known internationally for its range of trucks that feature traction to every wheel. The big, red and silver logo is most familiar in central Europe, although one or two Tatras are in the UK, and official imports may start soon.

I-SPY points: 45

Date: _____

TESLA

The Tesla was conceived in California, where internet millionaires had the idea of making an environmentally-friendly electric sports car powered by lithium-ion batteries (bigger versions of those used in mobile phones). It is built for Tesla by Lotus, and is now on sale in the UK. Serbian-born Nikola Tesla, who died in 1943, was a pioneering electrical inventor, after whom the two-seater roadster is named.

I-SPY points: 40

Date: _____

I-SPY points: 10

Date: _____

TOYOTA

Toyota is probably the most successful car brand of all time, taking the Japanese company from 1950s obscurity to become the world's biggest manufacturer today. In 1989, Toyota launched this new logo, consisting of three ellipses. Two of them intersect to form a kind of 'T', standing for Toyota, while an outer one encircles an empty background, suggesting the limitless opportunities available to the company.

I-SPY points: 45

Date: _____

TRABANT

On the bonnet of the Trabant – the only small car available to citizens of communist East Germany until the fall of the Berlin Wall in 1989 – is a large capital 'S' in a ring. Why? The tiny cars, now collectors' items, were built in the VEB Sachsenring Automobilwerke factory, Sachsenring being the name of a nearby racing circuit...and provider of that mystery 'S' initial.

TRIUMPH

This circular decal served as Triumph's logo from 1975, when the graphic victory laurels could be found on sporty cars like the Spitfire, TR7, and Dolomite saloon. Previously, Triumphs used logos featuring symbols of the globe or a bizarre 'open book' design; score for any Triumph logo you see. The last Triumph car was sold in 1984, so these are mostly classic cars today.

I-SPY points: 25

Date:

TVR

The three initials are seen linked together in this simple script on the low-slung bonnets of a wide range of high-performance sports cars. The last TVR was made in 2006, in Blackpool, but the enthusiasts who own them still grab every opportunity they can to enjoy them on British roads. The letters are a contraction of TreVoR, from Trevor Wilkinson, the man who founded the company.

I-SPY points: 20

Date:

I-SPY points: 10

Date: _____

VAUXHALL

This circular badge has a chromed metal surround, a black background and a silver design showing a griffin. This imaginary creature, a lion crossed with an eagle, holds a flag with the letter 'V' on it. Designed originally by employee Henry Varley in 1915, it was derived from the family crest of 13th century nobleman Fulk le Breant whose London home, Fulk's Hall, became Fawkes Hall, Foxhall and ultimately Vauxhall, where the carmaker was founded in 1903.

VOLKSWAGEN

Possibly the best-known car logo of all, but where the delightfully simple VW icon actually originated remains a mystery. Volkswagen's literal translation in English is 'Peoples Car' and was originally started to provide the people of Germany an affordable car in the 1930s, and appeared on the VW Beetle, a model still made today.

I-SPY points: 10

Date: _____

VOLVO

A circle with an arrow pointing diagonally out of its top-right corner is the mapping symbol for iron. It was selected by the founders of Volvo in 1927, because it fitted perfectly with their intention to build cars that were extremely sturdy. The logo has been refreshed several times over the years but is still faithful to the original design. Volvo, by the way, is Latin for 'I roll'.

I-SPY points: 10
Date:

I-SPY points: 30
Date:

WESTFIELD

This British make of two-seater sports cars has been on sale since 1983, and has always borne a circular logo featuring an Art Deco-style sunset. Many owners enjoy driving the cars on the road and at weekend motor sport events – and even building them, as Westfields can be purchased as a kit for assembly at home. Over 10,000 examples have been sold.

WOLSELEY

Between 1932 and 1976, Britain's upmarket Wolseley cars could boast a radiator badge that was truly unique. In cream plastic, with 'WOLSELEY' picked out in red, it was the only logo in the world that was illuminated at night. When the headlights were switched on, the logo came alive too! Sadly, this feature didn't stop the cars, considered rather old-fashioned, from losing popularity, and eventually dying out.

I-SPY points: 30

Date: _____

I-SPY points: 40

Date: _____

ZAGATO

You may be fortunate enough to see a sports car carrying this spiky 'Z' emblem. If so, it will feature bodywork designed and built by the Italian design company. It has created special versions of such cars as Alfa Romeos, Aston Martins and Lancias. They are highly sought after by collectors, so you might have to go to a classic car show or rally to spy a Zagato-bodied car.

Index

Michelin, Proprietaires-Editeurs 2010. Michelin and the
Michelin Man are registered Trademarks of Michelin.
Created and produced by Blue Sky Publishing Limited.
All rights reserved. No part of this publication may be
reproduced, copied or transmitted in any form without
the prior consent of the publisher.
The publisher gratefully acknowledges the contribution
of the I-Spy team: Camilla Lovell and Faron Watts in the
production of this title.
The publisher gratefully acknowledges the contribution
of Giles Chapman, who compiled the contents and
wrote the text.
The majority of the photographs are sourced from
the manufacturers. The publisher also gratefully
acknowledges, in particular, the helpful assistance of
Rosy Frost (Coleman Milne), David Hill of Ford (Ghia),
Aimi McNeill (Ginetta), Simon Saunders (Ariel), Nicola
Dandridge (Perouda) and Amy Wong of
Goingreen (Reva) for assistance in sourcing relevant
images. The photos for AC, Austin, Bristol,
Morris, Triumph and Wolseley are © James Mann
(www.jamesmann.com), used with thanks. The
Metrocab picture was taken by Annabel Chapman,
with thanks. Additional photographs were supplied by
the Giles Chapman Library and Unitaw Limited. Other
images in the public domain and used under a creative
commons licence.
Reprinted 2012   13 12 11 10 9 8 7

HOW TO GET YOUR I-SPY CERTIFICATE AND BADGE

Every time you score 1000 points or more in an I-Spy book, you can apply for a certificate

Here's what to do, step by step:

Certificate

- Ask an adult to check your score
- Ask his or her permission to apply for a certificate
- Apply online to www.ispymichelin.com
- Enter your name and address and the completed title
- We will send you back via e mail your certificate for the title

Badge

- Each I-Spy title has a cut out (page corner) token at the back of the book
- Collect five tokens from different I-Spy titles
- Put Second Class Stamps on two strong envelopes
- Write your own address on one envelope and put a £1 coin inside it (for protection). Fold, but do not seal the envelope, and place it inside the second envelope
- Write the following address on the second envelope, seal it carefully and post to:

I-Spy Books
Michelin Maps and Guides
Hannay House
39 Clarendon Road
Watford
WD17 1JA